THE 7 HABITS
ON THE GO

Also from FranklinCovey

THE 7 HABITS ON THE GO

Timeless Wisdom for a Rapidly Changing World

Inspired by the wisdom
of Stephen R. Covey

By Sean Covey

CORAL GABLES

Published by Mango Publishing Group, a division of
Mango Media Inc.

Mango is an active supporter of authors' rights to
free speech and artistic expression in their books. The
purpose of copyright is to encourage authors to produce
exceptional works that enrich our culture and our open
society.

Uploading or distributing photos, scans or any content
from this book without prior permission is theft of the
author's intellectual property. Please honor the author's
work as you would your own. Thank you in advance for
respecting our author's rights.

Content design, research, and editing: Annie Oswald and
Natasha Vera.

For permission requests, please contact:
FranklinCovey Co.
2200 W. Parkway Blvd.
Salt Lake City, UT 84119
Attn: Annie Oswald

For special orders, quantity sales, course adoptions
and corporate sales, please email the publisher at
sales@mango.bz. For trade and wholesale sales, please
contact Ingram Publisher Services at customer.service@
ingramcontent.com or +1.800.509.4887.

*The 7 Habits on the Go: Timeless Wisdom for a Rapidly
Changing World, Inspired by the Wisdom of Stephen R.
Covey*

ISBN: (p) 978-1-64250-435 4 (e) 978-1-64250-436-1

BISAC: BUS071000 BUSINESS & ECONOMICS / Leadership

Printed in the United States of America

"People can't live with change if there's not a changeless core inside them."

—Stephen R. Covey

Table of Contents

HABIT 6: SYNERGIZE

HABIT 7: SHARPEN THE SAW

BONUS FEATURES

Foreword

In my nearly twenty-five years working with the FranklinCovey company, the world leader in performance improvement, it never ceases to amaze me how many people around the world refer to our co-founder, Dr. Stephen R. Covey's seminal book—*The 7 Habits of Highly Effective People*—as *The 7 Habits of Highly* Successful *People* or The *7 Habits of Highly* Efficient *People*. To those who get the title wrong, it may seem like a minor difference, but in fact, Dr. Covey was quite deliberate and intentional about why he referred to these as being the habits of effective people.

Everything Dr. Covey worked for was geared towards building people's effectiveness, so, it's important not to lose the gravity of that—the deliberation and intentionality of his passion and legacy to help people grow in their effectiveness, not only with themselves, but in their interactions with others.

The first three habits focus on how to be effective in your own life; they are about the "private victory," the victory with self. Mastery over your own behaviors, attitude, priorities, mission, and purpose. The next three habits concern our interactions with others. The "public victory" relates to our interpersonal relationships, as a parent, spouse, leader, friend, colleague, or neighbor. As for the last habit, it is about renewal, and it encompasses all the others.

When it comes to *The 7 Habits*, my big *aha* moment involved Dr. Covey's articulation of the difference between "being efficient" and "being effective." It's an important distinction that shouldn't be lost on anybody—this difference between having an *efficient* mindset, and having an *effective* mindset.

I've always been a very efficient person. Anybody who knows me is aware that I get up early in the morning, at 4 a.m., to write articles and work on the chapters of my books. I also like lists. For example, a typical Saturday for me is highly efficient. By 9 a.m. I've washed my cars, run to Home Depot to buy yard supplies, mowed the lawn, and showered, ready to start the day. By most people's accounts, I'm hyper productive. I like to do things fast, and in great volume, and it's worked very well for me in most areas of my life, including my career.

I don't want you to think I am knocking down being efficient. No, efficiency is a great quality to have in your life. Many highly accomplished people are, in fact, very efficient. You can be efficient in meetings, with processes, texting, and email; taking out the garbage, and raking the lawn. There are lots of ways to be efficient. The problem is, I've taken on that efficiency paradigm—an efficiency mindset, if you will—and for most of my life I've replicated it into my relationships, personally and professionally, often to poor results.

Thanks to *The 7 Habits*, I had my own epiphany: You cannot be *efficient* in your relationships. In his book, Dr. Covey talked about how effective people don't try to be efficient in their relationships. There's a time for each, and for me, the biggest lesson with *The 7 Habits* is understanding when I should be operating in an efficiency mindset, and when I should be employing an effectiveness mindset. I think one of Dr. Covey's greatest quotes is: "With people, slow is fast, and fast is slow." You have to slow down, take your time, and listen empathically to build high-trust, enduring relationships.

As a leader, formal or informal, when someone comes to you and wants to connect with you on an issue, you might consider closing your laptop, taking off your glasses, turning off your phone, and really checking in with the person standing or sitting across from you. This idea that people are an organization's most valuable asset is bunk. It's simply not true. People are not an organization's most valuable asset. Rather it's the relationships *between* these people that creates culture and your competitive advantage.

Let me repeat: you cannot be efficient with people. And that's been my biggest lesson. I really appreciate the fact that I've tried to apply my biggest talent—efficiency—to everything, only to realize, "Oh, perhaps that's why some of my relationships aren't working out well, or I have conflict in my life. Perhaps that's why some people occasionally find me to be short, or rude, or not focused." Until I read Dr. Covey's book, I didn't understand that my talent in one area of my life was actually a liability in another area. It was hindering me from developing deep, trusting relationships with people. And, as I became a spouse and parent, it's become much clearer to me that any relationship rooted in an effectiveness mindset is much more enduring, beneficial, reciprocal, and meaningful.

So, what do I hope that the readers will get from this particular version of the book that changed my life? Everybody is trying to be very productive these days. Our fast world demands that we multitask, and a lot of us are doing more than is feasible or wise; in this context, *The 7 Habits on the Go* recognizes that not everyone has the ability nor the time to read, or reread, the full-length book. This is a chance to take some of the key insights Dr. Covey was so adept at condensing into short phrases, pointed terms, and quotes, and allow people to benefit from an easy, quick reference guide, that doesn't lack any of the profoundness. *The 7 Habits on the Go* is about accessibility. It's a little lighter primer to access these profound principles in an easy to read, easy to adopt format.

May this book help you acknowledge that the most important parts of your life are always rooted in your relationships, and that we all need to be aware of the importance of focusing on *effectiveness* versus *efficiency* in our relationships.

––––––––––––––––––

SCOTT JEFFREY MILLER

Author of *Management Mess to Leadership Success*

––––––––––––––––––

Introduction

Welcome to *The 7 Habits on the Go: Timeless Wisdom for a Rapidly Changing World.* Over the next week, month, or year—whatever amount of time you want to devote to this journey—I'm inviting you to move out of your comfort zone, shift your paradigms, improve and repair your relationships, and to generally become a more effective individual, personally and professionally.

You're probably thinking, "Yeah, right, Sean. I have so much going on right now—I don't have time to take on one more thing." But that's the very reason we created this book. It is on the go, quick, and effective. Just take a few minutes a day to read a section, then ask yourself the question of the week (stop and think about it too), and accept the challenge. The secret to improving yourself is not in making drastic changes overnight. It's in creating mini wins for yourself every day. If you spend a few minutes every day trying to be better than yesterday, you will reach your goals.

Each day you can steal a few moments to take in

important wisdom, all taken from the internationally bestselling book *The 7 Habits of Highly Effective People*, written by my father, Stephen R. Covey. This is a short book, but the lessons within are no less insightful. Each page teaches a key principle of effectiveness, poses a challenge, encourages reflection, and offers a quote of encouragement.

If you're the kind of person who prefers to skip around, that's just fine. Do it your way. Maybe read while you're waiting for a ride, while you're standing in line at the DMV, or downloading a movie—just stick with it—you'll be glad you did.

The best way to gain control of your life is to make a promise to yourself and then keep it. As you embark upon this journey and follow this simple process and begin making and keeping promises to yourself and others, you will increase your capacity to overcome challenges at work and at home. Never forget that out of small things, big things are achieved.

I wish you all the best on your journey.

SEAN COVEY

Author of *The 7 Habits of Highly Effective Teens* **and** *The 4 Disciplines of Execution*

THE 7 HABITS ON THE GO:

Introduction to the Habits

Define
Effectiveness

☐ List some things you would like to change
to become more effective. Keep this
list handy as you work through the
challenges in this book.

Ask yourself:

What matters most to me in my work and personal life?

When you shift your focus, you shift your impact. Put a spotlight on what matters in your life and list the next steps toward making positive change happen in those areas.

"If you apply even one of the 7 Habits today, you can see immediate results; but it's a lifetime adventure—a lifetime promise."

—Stephen R. Covey

Model Good Character

- ☐ Think of a person with excellent character.
- ☐ Define some of the principles they live by.
- ☐ Which of those principles would you like to implement?
- ☐ Do something today to act on those principles.

Introduction to the Habits

Ask yourself:

Have I focused on quick fixes at the expense of my character?

Like the top of a tree, our personality is what people see first. Although appearance, techniques, and skills can influence our success, the real source of lasting effectiveness lies in a strong character—the roots.

"People who live by the character ethic have strong roots, deep roots. They withstand the stresses of life, and they keep growing and progressing."

—Stephen R. Covey

Check Your Paradigms

- [ ] List five words that describe how you feel about an important aspect of your life.
- [ ] What do these words tell you about your paradigm?
- [ ] Identify how your paradigm needs to change to achieve your goals.

Introduction to the Habits

Ask yourself:

How accurate are my paradigms?

Paradigms are the way we see, understand, and interpret the world—our mental map.

"If you want to make minor changes in your life, work on your behavior. But if you want to make significant, quantum breakthroughs, work on your paradigms."

—Stephen R. Covey

HABIT 1:

Be Proactive

Take responsibility for your life.
You are not a victim of genetics,
circumstance, or upbringing. Live
life from your Circle of Influence.

Pause Between Stimulus and Response

- ☐ Think about the day ahead of you and anticipate one thing that might push your reactive buttons.
- ☐ Decide now what you can do to be proactive.

How could I respond proactively the next time I face a highly charged situation?

When people are reactive, they allow outside influences to control their response.

When people are proactive, they pause to allow themselves to choose their response based on principles and desired results.

"Between what happens to us and our response is a space, and the key to our growth and happiness is how we use that space."

—Stephen R. Covey

Become a Transition Person

- ☐ Think through the negative patterns that might have been passed on to you—a bad habit, negative attitude, etc.
- ☐ How are those things affecting you?
- ☐ Do something today to break the pattern.

Who has been a Transition Person for me? What influence did they have on my life?

A Transition Person breaks unhealthy, abusive, or ineffective behavior and passes on habits that strengthen and build others.

"You are influenced by your genes, by your upbringing, and by your environment, but you are not determined by them."

—Stephen R. Covey

Banish Reactive Language

☐ Try going an entire day without using any reactive language like "I can't" or "I have to" or "You make me so mad."

Ask yourself:

Are my words making me a victim?

Reactive language is a sure sign that you see yourself as a victim of circumstances, instead of as a proactive, self-reliant person.

"A serious problem with reactive language is that it becomes a self-fulfilling prophecy. People...feel victimized and out of control, not in charge of their life or their destiny. They blame outside forces—other people, circumstances, even the stars—for their own situation."

—Stephen R. Covey

Speak Proactively

☐ Consciously use these sentence starters today:
"I choose to..."
"I get to..."
"I can..."

Ask yourself:

How differently do I feel about myself when I use proactive language?

Our language is a real indicator of the degree to which we see ourselves as proactive people. Using proactive language helps us feel more capable and empowers us to act.

"I am not the product of my circumstances. I am a product of my decisions."

—Stephen R. Covey

Shrink Your Circle of Concern

☐ Think of a problem or opportunity you're currently facing.

☐ List everything within your Circle of Concern—and then let it go.

Ask yourself:

How much time and energy do I waste on things I can't control?

Your Circle of Concern includes things you worry about but can't control. If you focus on it, you have less time and energy to spend on things you can influence.

"Be a light, not a judge. Be a model, not a critic."

—Stephen R. Covey

Expand Your Circle of Influence

- ☐ Think of a big challenge you're facing.
- ☐ List everything you can control.
- ☐ Determine which action you will take today.

Ask yourself:

Is my Circle of Influence growing or shrinking?

Your Circle of Influence includes those things you can affect directly. When you focus on it, you expand your knowledge and experience. As a result, your Circle of Influence grows.

"Proactive people focus their efforts on the Circle of Influence. Their energy is positive, enlarging, and magnifying."

—Stephen R. Covey

Have a Proactive Day

☐ Today, summon one of the four endowments—self-awareness, conscience, indepedent will, and imagination—when you feel yourself becoming reactive. Try to use each one over the course of the day.

Ask yourself:

What's going on in my life today that might affect my proactivity?

Proactive people are the "creative force of their own lives"—they choose their own way and take responsibility for the results. Reactive people see themselves as victims.

"Every human being has four endowments—self-awareness, conscience, independent will, and creative imagination. These give us the ultimate human freedom: the power to choose."

—Stephen R. Covey

Begin With the End in Mind

Define your values, mission, and goals in life. Live based upon *your* vision of your life.

Define Outcomes Before You Act

☐ From today's schedule, pick one personal item and one work item. Write your end in mind for each one.

Ask yourself:

How are my outcomes different when I begin with a clear end in mind?

All things are created twice: a mental creation and a physical creation. Before you act, start with a clear idea of what you want to achieve.

"It's incredibly easy to work harder and harder at climbing the ladder of success, only to discover that it's leaning against the wrong wall."

—Stephen R. Covey

Celebrate Your 80th Birthday

□ Visualize your 80th birthday party. Write what you would like each person to say about you and the impact you've had on their life.

□ What one thing can you do this week to help make it a reality?

Ask yourself:

What legacy do I want to leave?

Being effective means taking the time to define the legacy you want to leave in your most important relationships and responsibilities.

"Deep within each one of us is an inner longing to live a life of greatness and contribution—to really matter, to really make a difference."

—Stephen R. Covey

Refine Your Mission Statement

☐ Write or revise your Personal Mission Statement. Check that it:
- Is based on principles.
- Clarifies what is important to you.
- Provides direction and purpose.
- Represents the best in you.

Ask yourself:

What is my compelling vision of my future?

Your mission statement defines your highest values and priorities. It's the end in mind for your life. It enables you to shape your future instead of letting it be shaped by other people or circumstances.

"The mission statement gives you a changeless sense of who you are."

—Stephen R. Covey

Rethink a Relationship

☐ Take time to write down your end in mind for an important relationship.

☐ Do something today to make that end in mind more of a reality.

This week, how can I tend to a relationship that matters most to me?

When we focus on efficiency, we sometimes overlook the people who really matter to us. But true effectiveness comes from the impact we have on others.

"How different our lives are when we really know what is deeply important to us."

—Stephen R. Covey

Share Your Mission Statement

☐ Today share your Personal Mission Statement with someone you trust—a friend or family member. Ask them to help you refine it.

Ask yourself:

Which people in my life are most affected by my personal mission?

Your mission statement is not just for you; your loved ones can benefit from knowing your goals, values, and vision.

"We detect rather than invent our missions in life."

—Viktor Frankl

Balance Your Roles

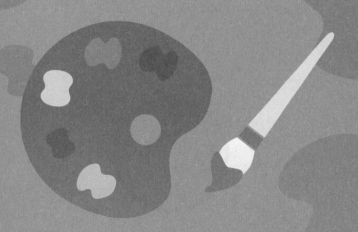

☐ Identify one of your most important roles
  in life—partner, professional, parent,
  neighbor, etc.—that you might be
  neglecting.

☐ Do something today to better fulfill that
  role.

Am I getting absorbed in one role to the disadvantage of the others?

In trying to fulfill all the key roles in our lives, we sometimes overemphasize one important role (often work-related) and get out of balance.

"One of the major problems that arises when people work to become more effective in life is that they...lose the sense of proportion, the balance...they may neglect the most precious relationships in their lives."

—Stephen R. Covey

HABIT 3:

Put First Things First

Prioritize your activities and focus on what matters most. Spend more of your time in Quadrant II: the quadrant of important but not urgent.

Set a Goal

- ☐ Consider a goal you've been working on or pick a new one. Define the outcome. What would success look like?
- ☐ In your planner, schedule the activities you need to progress your goal.

Ask yourself:

What one thing can I do that, if done regularly, would make a tremendous, positive influence in my life?

Your goals should reflect your deepest values, your unique talent, and your sense of mission. An effective goal gives meaning and purpose to your everyday life and translates into daily activities.

"Happiness—in part—is the fruit of the desire and ability to sacrifice what we want now for what we want eventually."

—Stephen R. Covey

Use Your Time Well

- ☐ At the start of the day, use the Time Matrix to estimate how many hours you will spend in each quadrant.

- ☐ At the end of the day, record how many hours you actually spent in each quadrant.

- ☐ Are you satisfied with how you spent your time? What needs to change?

Ask yourself:

Which quadrant do I spend most of my time in? What are the consequences?

The Time Matrix defines activities based on urgency and importance.

	URGENT	NOT URGENT
IMPORTANT	**Q1** NECESSITY Crises Emergency meetings Last-minute deadlines Pressing problems Unforeseen events	**Q2** EFFECTIVENESS Proactive work Important goals Creative thinking Planning and prevention Relationship building Learning and renewal Recreation

NOT IMPORTANT	**Q3** DISTRACTION
	
	Needless interruptions
	Unnecessary reports
	Irrelevant meetings
	Other people's minor issues
	Unimportant email,
	  tasks, phone calls, status
	  posts, etc.
		Q4 WASTE
		
		Trivial work
		Avoidance activities
		Excessive relaxation,
		  television, gaming,
		  Internet
		Time-wasters
		Gossip

"The key is not to prioritize what's on your schedule, but to schedule your priorities."

—Stephen R. Covey

Prepare for Quadrant 1

☐ Pick a recent Q1 urgency.
☐ Brainstorm ways you could avoid or prevent it in the future.

How many of my crises could be prevented with preparation?

Quadrant 1 is both urgent and important. It deals with the things that require immediate attention. We all have some Q1 activities in our lives, but some people are consumed by it.

"Most of us spend too much time on what is urgent and not enough time on what is important."

—Stephen R. Covey

Live in Quadrant 2

- [ ] Choose a Q2 activity that could have a significant impact on your life.
- [ ] Schedule time this week to do it.

Which Q2 activity do I most need to implement?

When we are highly effective, we spend most of our time in Quadrant 2:

- Proactive work
- Important goals
- Creative thinking
- Planning and preparing
- Building relationships
- Renewal and recreation

"The main thing is to keep the main thing the main thing."

—Stephen R. Covey

Plan Your Week

- ☐ Find a quiet place to plan for 20-30 minutes.
- ☐ Connect with your mission, roles, and goals.
- ☐ Choose one or two Big Rocks for each role and schedule them.
- ☐ Organize the rest of your tasks, appointments, and activities around your Big Rocks.

Habit 3: Put First Things First

Ask yourself:

What are the one or two most important things I can do in each role this week?

Effective people plan every week, taking time alone before the week begins. Your goals, roles, and Q2 activities are your "Big Rocks"—schedule them first and the "gravel" of less-important tasks will fit around them.

"If you were to ask me what single practice would do more than any other to balance your life and increase your productivity, it would be this: Plan your week...before the week begins."

—Stephen R. Covey

Stay True in the Moment of Choice

- ☐ Think of a situation when you find it hard to stay true in the moment of choice.
- ☐ Figure out a tactic you can use to achieve your Q2 priorities in that moment.

Ask yourself:

What pulls me away from following through on my Big Rocks? How do I feel when I give in to the pressures and neglect my true priorities?

Our character is revealed when we choose between our Q2 priorities and the pressures of the moment. We are effective when we align our choices with our mission, roles, and goals.

"As you go through your week...the urgent but not important will threaten to overpower the important Quadrant 2 activities you planned. Use your independent will and maintain your integrity to the truly important."

—Stephen R. Covey

Eliminate the Unimportant

☐ Make a list of timewasters and distractions.

☐ Circle the one that is the biggest culprit.

☐ Do something today to eliminate or cut back on it.

Ask yourself:

How much time am I spending in Quadrants 3 and 4? What price am I paying to stay there?

Quadrants 3 and 4 are time robbers: activities that steal time from you without giving back.

"You have to decide what your highest priorities are and have the courage—pleasantly, unapologetically—to say 'no' to other things. And the way you do that is by having a bigger 'yes' burning inside."

—Stephen R. Covey

Keep Your Commitments

- ☐ Think of an important goal that you haven't made progress on.

- ☐ Think of the smallest possible action you could take to progress that goal.

- ☐ Keep your commitment no matter what. Next week, take on a slightly larger goal.

Ask yourself:

Do I trust myself to follow through on the commitments I make to myself?

Most goals are challenging—otherwise we would have accomplished them already! We can become frustrated with ourselves if we truly want to accomplish a goal but continue to procrastinate acting on it.

"Make a little promise to yourself and keep it; then a little bigger one, then a bigger one. Eventually, your sense of honor will become greater than your moods."

—Stephen R. Covey

Private Victory to Public Victory

Build Your Emotional Bank Accounts

- ☐ Identify an important relationship that might be in disrepair.
- ☐ List three deposits you could make.
- ☐ List three withdrawals you need to avoid.

Do I know what constitutes withdrawals and deposits for the important people in my life?

The Emotional Bank Account symbolizes the amount of trust that exists in a relationship. Deposits build and repair trust. Withdrawals break down trust.

"In relationships, the little things are the big things."

—Stephen R. Covey

Apologize

☐ Apologize to someone you've wronged. Find out what you can do to repair the harm.

Ask yourself:

Who needs an apology from me?

Saying you're sorry when you've made a mistake or hurt someone can quickly restore an overdrawn Emotional Bank Account. It takes courage.

"To rebuild broken relationships, we must first study our own hearts to discover our own responsibilities, our own faults."

—Stephen R. Covey

Forgive

- [ ] If you've been hurt and it still bothers you, realize that person has weaknesses just as you do.
- [ ] Forgive that person.

Ask yourself:

Am I carrying around the burden of someone else's words or actions?

We've all been hurt at some time or another by someone else's thoughtless words or actions.

"Any time we think the problem is 'out there,' that very thought is the problem."

—Stephen R. Covey

HABIT 4:

Think
Win-Win

Have an everyone-can-win
attitude; be happy for the success
of others.

Consider Other People's Wins as Well as Your Own

☐ Pick an important relationship that could benefit from win-win thinking.

☐ Write down your wins and the other person's wins. Don't know what they would consider a win? Ask!

Ask yourself:

In what relationships are you less likely to Think Win, Win? What benefits would come from considering their wins?

When we are highly effective, we value other people's wins equally to our own. We take time to identify both our wins and their wins.

"Win-win is not a technique; it's a total philosophy of human interaction. It is a frame of mind and heart that seeks mutual benefit in all interactions. Win-win sees life as a cooperative, not a competitive, arena."

—Stephen R. Covey

Avoid the Scarcity Mentality

- ☐ List the areas of your life where you have a Scarcity Mentality (that there is not enough love, money, attention, resources, to go around).

- ☐ Consider where this Scarcity Mentality might come from.

Where is scarcity thinking getting in the way of achieving my best results?

The Scarcity Mentality causes you to compare, compete, and feel threatened by others, instead of working *with* others for the biggest wins.

"Most people are deeply scripted in the Scarcity Mentality. They see life as having only so much, as though there were only one pie out there. And if someone else gets a big piece of pie, it means less for everybody else."

—Stephen R. Covey

Cultivate an Abundance Mentality

☐ Describe what you could do to think more abundantly: celebrate the strengths of yourself and others, stop comparing, and share resources.

Ask yourself:

Do I truly believe that there is more than enough for everyone?

When we have an Abundance Mentality, we are not threatened by others' success, because we are secure in our own self-worth.

"The Abundance Mentality flows out of a deep inner sense of personal worth and security. It is the paradigm that there is plenty out there and enough for everybody."

—Stephen R. Covey

Balance Courage and Consideration

☐ Pick an issue where you would like to have more courage. Write down your point of view. Share your ideas and opinions with confidence.

☐ Pick a situation where you need to demonstrate more consideration. Focus on acknowledging others, not interrupting, and making sure everyone has a chance to be heard.

Ask yourself:

Are there relationships in which you lack courage or consideration? What price are you paying?

To be highly effective means to be courageous. We are willing and able to speak our thoughts respectfully. It also means being considerate. We are willing and able to seek out and listen to others' thoughts and feelings with respect.

"If people can express their feelings and convictions with courage balanced with consideration for the feelings and convictions of others, they are mature, particularly if the issue is very important to both parties."

—Stephen R. Covey

Make a Win-Win Agreement

☐ Choose a relationship that could benefit from a Win-Win Agreement. Write down what you think would be wins for that person—or ask them. Write down your own wins.

☐ Make a Win-Win Agreement.

What is my intent when I negotiate with others? Am I committed to win-win?

In a Win-Win Agreement, people commit to work to benefit both parties. Win-Win Agreements can be formal or informal and can be made in any relationship or circumstance.

"An agreement means very little in letter without the character and relationship to sustain it in spirit. We need to approach win-win from a genuine desire to invest in the relationships that make it possible."

—Stephen R. Covey

Give Credit

☐ Identify someone who deserves credit
for something they've done or helped
you accomplish. Privately or publicly
acknowledge that person's contribution.

Ask yourself:

Who has recently helped me accomplish something? Have I thanked them?

For many people, public or private acknowledgement is a big win. We can build trust and strengthen our relationships when we share credit generously.

"It's amazing how much you can accomplish when it doesn't matter who gets the credit."

—Harry S. Truman

HABIT 5:

Seek First to Understand, Then to Be Understood

Listen to people empathically and then ask to be heard.

Practice Empathic Listening

- [ ] Today practice listening for understanding.
- [ ] Try to reflect back the feelings of others and the content of the message. Check yourself when you interrupt, give advice, or judge.

Ask yourself:

Do people around me feel that I genuinely understand them?

Listening with empathy means getting to the heart of what matters to the other person, whether we agree or not. When listening empathically, we listen with the intent to understand. We respond by reflecting feelings and words.

"Next to human survival, the greatest need of a human being is psychological survival—to be understood, to be affirmed, to be validated, to be appreciated."

—Stephen R. Covey

Open Your Heart

☐ Identify someone you don't listen to closely and simply ask, "How's it going?" Open your heart and practice empathic listening. You'll be surprised at what you learn.

Am I truly listening to those I love?

When emotions are high, focus on your intent; don't worry about the correct response.

"When you really listen to another person from their point of view, and reflect back to them that understanding, it's like giving them emotional oxygen."

—Stephen R. Covey

Avoid
Autobiographical
Listening

☐ Think of a time when someone listened to
you with understanding and respect. How
did you feel?

Do I listen with the intent to reply, rather than to understand?

Autobiographical listening is filtering what others say through your own story. Rather than focusing on the speaker, you're waiting to jump in with your perspective.

"Listen, or your tongue will make you deaf."

—Native American Proverb

Seek to Be Understood

- ☐ Think about an upcoming presentation or persuasive message you need to give.
- ☐ Make sure you first understand others' points of view.
- ☐ Practice delivering your opinion with courage and consideration for others' views.

Ask yourself:

Do I speak in a way that shows I understand the other person? Am I sharing my point of view clearly?

Seeking to understand is the second half of effective communication. Once we are confident others feel understood, we can share our point of view with respect and clarity.

"When you present your own ideas clearly in the context of a deep understanding of the other person's paradigms and concerns, you increase the credibility of your ideas."

—Stephen R. Covey

Bring Empathic Communication to the Digital World

☐ The next time you digitally communicate when emotions are high, try using one of these:

- Allow the other person to finish their thoughts before responding.
- Reflect their feelings and words before expressing your own.
- Clearly state your intent: be specific.

Ask yourself:

How can I listen with empathy during text, phone, and email conversations?

Effective communication in the digital world requires the same intent and skills used in face-to-face communication. The challenge often lies in reading and relaying intent across media.

"Empathy is the fastest form of human communication."

—Stephen R. Covey

Synergize

Value and celebrate differences
so that you can achieve more
than you ever could have alone.

Learn from Differences

- ☐ Choose a political or social issue you care about.
- ☐ Put your personal views aside.
- ☐ Find a few people and find out their views. Listen for understanding.
- ☐ Write down at least three new perspectives you got from this exercise.

What can I learn from those I disagree with?

We have tremendous opportunity to grow from others' experiences, points of view, and wisdom. Differences can be a source of learning, rather than conflict.

"Insecure people have a need to mold them into their own thinking. They don't realize that the very strength of the relationship is in having another point of view. Sameness is uncreative—and boring."

—Stephen R. Covey

Solve a Problem with Synergy

☐ Find someone (or a group) to talk to about a problem you're facing.

☐ Ask, "Would you help me come up with ideas I haven't thought of yet?"

☐ Take a few minutes to brainstorm. Which ideas can you use?

Ask yourself:

What problem seems insurmountable if I face it alone?

You don't have to figure out all the answers by yourself. When you're dealing with a problem, synergy can surface ideas you never would have come up with on your own.

"Alone we can do so little; together we can do so much."

—Helen Keller

Seek 3rd Alternatives

☐ Observe an upcoming meeting and identify if synergy is or isn't occurring.

☐ Think of a problem that would benefit from synergy. Use it to seek a 3rd Alternative.

Ask yourself:

When am I likely to settle for compromise? When do I experience synergy? What's the difference?

Synergy depends on a willingness to seek a 3rd Alternative. More than just "my way" or "your way" it's a higher, better way. It's something that neither of us would have come up with on our own.

"What is synergy? Simply defined, it means that the whole is greater than the sum of its parts. Synergy means that one plus one may equal ten, or a hundred, or even a thousand!"

—Stephen R. Covey

Value Differences

- ☐ Identify someone you disagree with and make a list of their strengths.

- ☐ When they disagree with you, say, "Great! You see things differently. I need to listen to you."

Do I know the unique strengths of the people I work and live with? In which relationships do I tolerate differences rather than value them?

Valuing differences is the foundation of synergy. We are effective when we value and embrace the differences rather than rejecting or merely tolerating them. We see others' differences as strengths, not weaknesses.

"The essence of synergy is to value differences—to respect them, to build on strengths, to compensate for weaknesses."

—Stephen R. Covey

Rate Your Openness to Differences

- ☐ List some differences that show up in your relationships: age, politics, style, etc.

- ☐ Write down what you could do to better value differences.

Ask yourself:

Am I open to learning from differences?

Our paradigm is often that we are objective, but everyone else isn't. Effectiveness requires the humility to recognize the limitations of our perceptions.

"The key to valuing differences is to realize that all people see the world, not as it is, but as they are."

—Stephen R. Covey

Take Down Barriers

☐ Think about a goal you're working on.

☐ Identify the obstacles you're facing.

☐ Find someone to help you brainstorm ways to overcome those obstacles.

Habit 6: Synergize

Ask yourself:

What obstacle currently seems insurmountable if I face it alone?

When you approach a problem with the willingness to synergize, you can come up with new ways to overcome challenges.

"When you introduce synergy...you unfreeze [restraining forces], loosen them up, and create new insights."

—Stephen R. Covey

Leverage the Strengths of Others

- [ ] List your closest friends, family, and colleagues.

- [ ] Next to each person's name, list their strengths.

- [ ] Could you match any of these strengths to a challenge you're facing?

Ask yourself:

What could I do to take greater advantage of the strengths of others in my life?

We are surrounded by the strengths of others, but we often don't tap into them.

"When we're left to our own experiences, we constantly suffer from a shortage of data."

—Stephen R. Covey

Sharpen the Saw

Consistently recharge your batteries in all four dimensions: physical, mental, spiritual, and social/emotional.

Achieve the Daily Private Victory

- [ ] Write your own routine for daily renewal. Where can you improve?
- [ ] Block out time for renewal in your next weekly planning.

Ask yourself:

Am I spending time each day renewing my body, mind, heart, and spirit?

The Daily Private Victory—time spent each day in a routine way renewing body, mind, heart, and spirit—is the key to developing all of the 7 Habits.

"There's no other way you could spend an hour that would begin to compare with the Daily Private Victory. It will affect every decision, every relationship. It will greatly improve the quality, the effectiveness, of every other hour of the day."

—Stephen R. Covey

Habit
7

Strengthen Your Body

☐ Choose one way to build your physical capacity this week:
  · Set your alarm—for bedtime.
  · Find a way to be active that challenges you.
  · Add a new component to your exercise routine: endurance, flexibility, or strength.

Ask yourself:

What's one way I could improve my strength and resilience?

Physical renewal involves caring for your physical body—a healthy diet, sufficient rest, and regular exercise.

"Most of us think we don't have enough time to exercise. What a distorted paradigm! We don't have time not to."

—Stephen R. Covey

Renew
Your Spirit

☐ Choose one way to build your spiritual
capacity this week:
· Refine your Personal Mission
  Statement.
· Spend time in nature.
· Listen to or create music.
· Volunteer in your community.

Ask yourself:

Am I centered on my values?

Spirituality is a very private area of life and a supremely important one. It draws on the sources that inspire and uplift you.

"The spiritual dimension is your core, your center, your commitment to your value system."

—Stephen R. Covey

Sharpen Your Mind

☐ Choose one way to build your mental capacity this week:
- Keep a journal.
- Read a classic.
- Develop a hobby.

Do I begin the week mentally refreshed?

As soon as we leave school, many of us let our minds atrophy. But learning is vital to mental renewal.

"There's no better way to inform and expand your mind on a regular basis than to get into the habit of reading good literature."

—Stephen R. Covey

Develop Your Heart

☐ Choose one way to build your social/
emotional capacity this week:
· Invite a friend to dinner.
· Forgive someone.
· Text or email a friend you haven't
heard from lately.

Ask yourself:

Who can I connect with this week?

Our emotional life is primarily—but not exclusively—developed through our relationships with other people.

"To touch the soul of another human being is to walk on holy ground."

—Stephen R. Covey

Take Time for Yourself

☐ Give yourself permission to take thirty minutes just for yourself today. Find a stressbuster and do it.

Are urgencies crowding out my renewal time?

Renewal is a Quadrant 2 activity; we must be proactive to make it happen.

"This is the single most powerful investment we can ever make in life—investment in ourselves."

—Stephen R. Covey

Tame Your Technology

☐ Do one thing today to reduce distractions from
technology:
- Turn off alerts.
- Check social media only once a day.
- Make a policy to never let your device
  interrupt a conversation.
- Turn off your devices while working on your
  Big Rocks.

Ask yourself:

Am I using my technology at the expense of my most important goals and relationships?

Our devices can be the ultimate source of urgencies. We might feel productive responding to every message, but mostly we're simply distracted.

"For all our efforts to manage our time, do more, be more, and achieve greater efficiency through the wonders of modern technology, why is it we often find ourselves in the 'thick of thin things'?"

—Stephen R. Covey

Bonus
Features

why or what drove me to focus on goals,
but somehow I did and just assumed that
everyone else did, too.".

This experience is likely not uncommon. The
are many who have not specifically defined
contribution they want to make in life, or
their driving purpose will be. For this reas
important to provide a means of doing
you have defined your life goals at an
like Annie, this could be an exercise th
you to stay on track. Who knows? Yo
even change.

Please enjoy the following though
as you read, ask yourself these q

- Have I defined my purpo
- Am I aware of what I u
  others can't or won't
- What and who do I w
- What principles and
  rny life by?
- What will be my

Mission Statement Builder

"How different our lives are when we really know what is deeply important to us, and, keeping that picture in mind, we manage ourselves each day to be and to do what really matters most."

—Stephen R. Covey

As I debated on what bonus features to add to this book, I asked myself, "What will have the greatest influence on my reader and on their future?" And then I remembered when my colleague, Annie, once shared this story:

"I taught the 7 Habits at a local community college for several years. It was an incredible experience helping these young people, and not-so-young, non-traditional students, about the power of habits, goals, and principles. As their teacher and friend, I was curious about the impact of the content and the habits on the students. I wanted to know where they felt the greatest connection and th

Use everything you learned in this book to help you build your mission statement and become the most effective person you can be. Your effectiveness can change the world.

THE EDITOR

"Writing or reviewing a mission statement changes you because it forces you to think through your priorities deeply, carefully, and to align your behavior with your beliefs. As you do, other people begin to sense that you're not being driven by everything that happens to you."

—Stephen R. Covey

return on their time by taking this class. S
I randomly added a 'freebie' question to
final exam. I wanted to give the student
opportunity to share honestly—and ev
should include a freebie question, sho
No one should totally fail every ques
test unless they simply don't take it

The question at the end of the fin
was, 'What is your favorite habit
I was very surprised to discover
overwhelming majority of the
Habit 2: Begin with the End in
reasons varied, but a centra
through: this was the first
students had plotted out
future. Some, not all, ha
college and what they
embrace as a professi
college only because
99 percent of my co
vision—no driving p
no life mission.

I was totally stu
semester, my s
at the end of
purpose and mea...

I think I was so surprised becu...
my life goals at a young age—I don't ..

Visualize Your Legacy

Before we get to the mission statement-building questionnaire, please find a place to read these next few pages where you can be alone and uninterrupted. Clear your mind of everything except what you will read and what I will invite you to do.

• • •

In your mind's eye, see yourself going to the funeral of a loved one. You see the faces of friends and family. You feel the shared sorrow that radiates from the hearts of the people there.

As you walk to the front of the room and look inside the casket, you suddenly come face to face with yourself. This is *your* funeral. All these people have come to honor you. As you wait for the service to begin, you look at the program and see there are to be four speakers.

The first is from your family. The second speaker is one of your friends. The third speaker is from your work. And the fourth is from your community.

Now think deeply. What would you like each of these speakers to say about you and your life?

"If you carefully consider what you
wanted to be said of you in the funeral
experience, you will find your definition
of success."

If you participated seriously in this visualization
experience, you touched for a moment on some
of your deep, fundamental values. You established
brief contact with that inner guidance system.

...

To Begin with the End in Mind means to start
with a clear understanding of your destination.
It means to know where you're going so that you
better understand where you are now and so that
the steps you take are always in the right direction.
This is something I once wrote about this habit:

"Habit 2, Begin with the End in Mind,
means developing a clear picture of where
you want to go with your life. It means
deciding what your values are and setting
goals. If Habit 1 says you are the driver of
your life, Habit 2 says decide where you
want to go and draw up a map to
get there."

How different our lives are when we really know what is deeply important to us, and, keeping that picture in mind, we manage ourselves each day to be and to do what matters most.

We each have a number of different roles in our lives—different areas or capacities in which we have responsibility. I may, for example, have a role as an individual, a husband, a father, a teacher, and a businessman. And each of these roles is important.

One of the major problems that arises when people work to become more effective in life is that they don't think broadly enough. They lose the sense of proportion, the balance, the natural ecology necessary to effective living. They may get consumed by work and neglect personal health. In the name of professional success, they may neglect the most precious relationships in their lives.

You may find that your mission statement will be much more balanced and much easier to work with, if you break it down into the specific role area of your life and the goals you want to accomplish in each other.

Writing your mission in terms of the important roles in your life gives you balance and harmony. It keeps each role clearly before you. You can review your roles frequently to make sure that you don't get totally absorbed by one role to the exclusion of others that are equally or even more important in your life.

After you identify your various roles, then you can think about the long-term goals you want to accomplish in each of those roles. We're into the right brain, using imagination, creativity, conscience, and inspiration. If these goals are the extension of a mission statement based on correct principles, they will be vitally different from the goals people normally set. They will be in harmony with correct principles, with natural laws, which gives you greater power to achieve them. They are not someone else's goals you have absorbed. They are *your* goals. They reflect your deepest values, your unique talent, your sense of mission.

"I think each of us has an internal monitor or sense, a conscience, that gives us an awareness of our own uniqueness and the singular contributions we can make."

statement by
who is it for,
journey's res

1) My life's

Step 6:

1) Imac
with y
them

Ste

1)
f

> An effective goal focuses primarily on results rather than activity. It identifies where you want to be, and, in the process, helps you determine where you are.
>
> Roles and goals give structure and organized direction to your personal mission. If you don't yet have a personal mission statement, it's a good place to begin. Simply identify the various areas of your life and the two or three important results you feel you should accomplish in each area to move ahead; this will give you an overall perspective of your life and a sense of direction.
>
> —— **STEPHEN R. COVEY**

• • •

FranklinCovey's personal mission statement builder will help you create a unique, personalized mission statement. To build your own Personal Mission Statement online, visit https://msb.franklincovey.com.

Let's begin.

Missio
Qu

Step 1: Perfo

1) I am at m

2) I am at

Step 2: F

1) Wha

2) Wh

Step

1)
b

Affirmations on the Go

Here are some affirmations to keep you focused on your mission, and remind you of the power of the habits. As you work on each habit, take one of these affirmations and repeat it to yourself throughout the day. Make it your focus, and watch your perspective change.

Habit 1: Be Proactive

My ability to conquer my challenges is limitless; my potential to succeed is infinite.

I wake up every morning feeling positive and enthusiastic about life.

I carry my own weather.

I am mindful of my language. I avoid reactive language.

I face my failures head-on. The only failure is giving up. I learn from my failures.

I recognize resistance as merely an obstacle, not a roadblock.

I face my fears head on. I learn from them.

I push pause and think before reacting to an emotional or difficult situation.

Habit 2: Begin with the End in Mind

I am willing to explore new and uncharted territory.

I am the architect of my life; I build its foundation and choose its contents.

I live by my mission. I follow the beat of my inner drummer. I will be myself, not what others want me to be.

I invest my time, talents, abilities, and life in those activities which fulfill my ultimate purpose.

I am the captain of my ship; I chart my own course and choose my own cargo.

I refer back to my mission statement whenever I am faced with important life decisions.

I frequently ask myself: "Is the life I'm living leading me in the right direction?"

Habit 3: Put First Things First

My mind is energized, clear, and focused on the process of my goals.

My daily goals will ensure I reach my long term goals.

For today, I am truly attentive to my work. I will be observant and attentive throughout the day.

Today I will spend time strengthening relationships.

I turn my dreams into goals. I turn my goals into steps. I turn my steps into actions. I complete an action every day.

I will prepare today for future crises.

I concentrate all my efforts on the things I want to accomplish in life.

I spend my time focused on what matters most.

Habit 4: Think Win-Win

I face difficult situations with a balance of courage and consideration. I will find solutions in these difficult times.

In seeking for Win-Win I focus on the issues, not the personalities or positions.

I am genuinely happy for the success of others.

My abundance mentality flows out of my own deep inner sense of personal worth and security.

I choose a Win-Win frame of mind and heart that constantly seeks mutual benefit in all human interaction.

I confidently practice Win-Win as a habit of interpersonal leadership.

When others are scripted in Win-Lose, I balance courage with consideration in finding mutual benefit.

Habit 5: Seek First to Understand, Then to Be Understood

I listen reflectively without judgment to gain complete understanding.

I choose to see things from another's point of view before sharing my own.

The deepest need of the human heart is to be understood.

I listen with my heart, my eyes, and then my ears.

I show my level of care and commitment by empathically listening.

I am mindful of timing and my choice of words when I give feedback.

I practice patience and understanding with others and myself.

Habit 6: Synergize

I am a problem solver. I work with others to find the very best solutions.

I celebrate diversity and I value differences in people and ideas.

In my personal relationships, I strive for the ideal environment for synergy—a high emotional bank account, think Win-Win, and seek first to understand.

I am committed to working with others to create a better solution.

I keep my mind open to the possibilities of teamwork and communication.

There is an abundance of benefit, recognition, and success to go around for everyone.

Habit 7: Sharpen the Saw

I am fit, healthy, and full of self-confidence. My outer self is matched by my inner well-being.

I have strength in my heart and clarity in my mind.

I seek balance in the four dimensions of my life: physical, mental, spiritual, and social/emotional.

I am calm and relaxed which energizes my whole being.

Life is an upward spiral of learn, commit, do, and learn, commit, and do over and over again.

My body is a marvelous machine. I handle it with care and I don't abuse it.

I look for ways to build others up rather than to tear them down.

I find peace and calm in nature.

I use my gift of imagination to clearly visualize the attainment of my goals.

7 Quick Takeaways from *The 7 Habits on the Go*

Habit 1: Be Proactive. Take responsibility for your life. You are not a victim of genetics, circumstance, or upbringing. Live life from your Circle of Influence.

Habit 2: Begin With the End in Mind. Define your values, mission, and goals in life. Live life based upon your vision of your life.

Habit 3: Prioritize your activities and focus on what matters most. Spend more of your time in Quadrant II: the quadrant of important but not urgent.

Habit 4: Think Win-Win. Have an everyone-can-win attitude; be happy for the success of others.

Habit 5: Seek First to Understand, Then to Be Understood. Listen to people empathically and then ask to be heard.

Habit 6: Synergize. Value and celebrate differences so that you can achieve more than you ever could have alone.

Habit 7: Sharpen the Saw. Consistently recharge your batteries in all four dimensions: physical, mental, spiritual, and social/emotional.

Stephen R. Covey

Dr. Stephen R. Covey passed away in 2012 leaving behind an unmatched legacy of teachings about leadership, time management, effectiveness, success, and love and family. A multimillion-copy bestselling author of self-help and business classics, Dr. Covey strove to help readers recognize the principles that would lead them to personal and professional effectiveness. His seminal work, *The 7 Habits of Highly Effective People*, transformed the way people think and act upon their problems with a compelling, logical, and well-defined process.

As an internationally respected leadership authority, family expert, teacher, organizational consultant, and author, his advice gives insight to millions. His books have sold more than 40 million copies (in 50 languages), and *The 7 Habits of Highly Effective People* was named the #1 Most Influential Business Book of the Twentieth Century. He was the author of *The 3rd Alternative*, *The 8th Habit*, *The Leader in Me*, *First Things First*, and many other titles. He held an MBA from Harvard and a doctorate from Brigham Young University. He lived with his wife and family in Utah.

FranklinCovey
ALL ACCESS PASS®

The FranklinCovey All Access Pass provides unlimited access to our best-in-class content and solutions, allowing you to expand your reach, achieve your business objectives, and sustainably impact performance across your organization.

AS A PASSHOLDER, YOU CAN:

- Access FranklinCovey's world-class content, whenever and wherever you need it, including *The 7 Habits of Highly Effective People®: Signature Edition 4.0*, Leading at the *Speed of Trust®*, and *The 5 Choices to Extraordinary Productivity®*.

- Certify your internal facilitators to teach our content, deploy FranklinCovey consultants, or use digital content to reach your learners with the behavior-changing content you require.

- Have access to a certified implementation specialist who will help design impact journeys for behavior change.

- Organize FranklinCovey content around your specific business-related needs.

- Build a common learning experience throughout your entire global organization with our core-content areas, localized into 16 languages.

Join thousands of organizations using the All Access Pass to implement strategy, close operational gaps, increase sales, drive customer loyalty, and improve employee engagement.

To learn more, visit
FRANKLINCOVEY.COM or call **1-888-868-1776**.

FranklinCovey.
THE ULTIMATE COMPETITIVE ADVANTAGE

FRANKLINCOVEY
ONLEADERSHIP
WITH
SCOTT MILLER

Join executive vice president Scott Miller
for weekly interviews with thought leaders,
bestselling authors, and world-renowned
experts on the topics of organizational culture,
leadership development, execution,
and personal productivity.

FEATURED INTERVIEWS INCLUDE:

GUY KAWASAKI
WISE GUY

KIM SCOTT
RADICAL CANDOR

SETH GODIN
THE DIP, LINCHPIN, PURPLE COW

LIZ WISEMAN
MULTIPLIERS

STEPHEN M. R. COVEY
THE SPEED OF TRUST

SUSAN CAIN
THE QUIET REVOLUTION

GENERAL STANLEY McCHRYSTAL
LEADERS: MYTH AND REALITY

SUSAN DAVID
EMOTIONAL AGILITY

DANIEL PINK
WHEN

JEAN CHATZKY
AGEPROOF

RACHEL HOLLIS
GIRL, WASH YOUR FACE

NANCY DUARTE
DATA STORY, SLIDE:OLOGY

STEPHANIE McMAHON
CHIEF BRAND OFFICER, WWE

CHRIS McCHESNEY
THE 4 DISCIPLINES
OF EXECUTION

Subscribe to FranklinCovey's *On Leadership*
to receive weekly videos, tools, articles,
and podcasts at

FRANKLINCOVEY.COM/ONLEADERSHIP.

TAKE THE NEXT STEP IN YOUR JOURNEY

PARTICIPATE IN A TWO-DAY *7 HABITS*® WORK SESSION

Continue your journey toward effectively leading yourself, engaging and collaborating with others, and continually improving and renewing your capabilities. *The 7 Habits of Highly Effective People®: Signature Edition 4.0* is renowned as the world's premier personal leadership-development work session.

In this two-day experience, you will learn how to:

- Have a proactive mindset and resist self-defeating reactivity driven by others' moods and external influences.
- Identify and align with your personal mission and core values.
- Adopt principles that will transform your daily productivity.
- Apply crucial listening skills that form the basis of effective communication.

To register or for more information, visit
FRANKLINCOVEY.COM/7HWORKSESSION
or call 1-888-868-1776.

FranklinCovey has partnered with American Management Association® to make this two-day work session available to you Live In-Person or Live-Online.

Mango Publishing, established in 2014, publishes an eclectic list of books by diverse authors—both new and established voices—on topics ranging from business, personal growth, women's empowerment, LGBTQ studies, health, and spirituality to history, popular culture, time management, decluttering, lifestyle, mental wellness, aging, and sustainable living. We were recently named 2019 and 2020's #1 fastest growing independent publisher by Publishers Weekly. Our success is driven by our main goal, which is to publish high quality books that will entertain readers as well as make a positive difference in their lives.

Our readers are our most important resource; we value your input, suggestions, and ideas. We'd love to hear from you—after all, we are publishing books for you!

Please stay in touch with us and follow us at:

Facebook: Mango Publishing

Twitter: @MangoPublishing

Instagram: @MangoPublishing

LinkedIn: Mango Publishing

Pinterest: Mango Publishing

Sign up for our newsletter at www.mangopublishinggroup.com and receive a free book!

Join us on Mango's journey to reinvent publishing, one book at a time.